Art in Action

Credits

Cover: Illustration by Judy Sakaguchi.

Art and Production: Book Production Systems, Inc.

Illustrations: Janet Colby, Jennifer Hewitson, Jannine Muelchi, Jim Staunton, Debra Stein. All illustrators represented by Richard W. Salzman, Artist Representative.

Publisher's Photos: All photos by Johnny Johnson/Click Studios except as credited below. Key: (t) top, (c) center, (b) bottom, (l) left, (r) right.

UNIT 1: Page viii(r), Debbie Dean; 1(t), Debra L. Saleny; 1(b), Budd Titlow/Naturegraphs; 2(l), Image Bank West/Pete Turner; 3(t), Larry Lee/West Light; 4(tl), D. Muench/ H. Armstrong Roberts; 4(tr), Camerique; 4(cl), Image Bank West/Robin Forbes; 4(cr), Steve Allen/Peter Arnold, Inc.; 4(bl), Chuck O'Rear/West Light; 4(br); Craig Aurness/West Light; 6(tl), Larry Lee/West Light; 6(tr), Bill Ross/West Light; 6(cl), Steven C. Kaufman/Peter Arnold, Inc.; 6(cr), E.R. Degginger; 6(bl), G.L. Kooyman; 7(tr), Art Resource, NY; 16, Bruno J. Zehnder, New York City; 18, Sydney D. Brown; 26(cl), William James Warren/West Light; 26(bl), Fritz Prenzel/Bruce Coleman, Inc.; 26(br), Four By Five; 28(tl), 28(bl), 28(br), Michael W. Green; 29(bl), Leven Leatherbury; 29(bc), 29(br), Barbara Herberholz; 31, Mike Neumann/National Audubon Society Collection/P.R.

UNIT 2: Page 36(t), Eliot Elisofon; 36(b), Image Bank West/Jurgen Schmitt; 40(tl), 40(tr), Grant Heilman/Grant Heilman Photography; 47, David Muench; 49(tl), Malcolm S. Kirk/Peter Arnold, Inc.; 49(tr), Rod Planck/Click, Chicago; 49(b), Leonard Lee Rue III/ Animals, Animals; 56, Barbara Herberholz.

UNIT 3: Page 67(t), Art Resource, NY; 68(b), Sydney D. Brown; 71(t), Leven Leatherbury; 72, Jay Maisel; 75(t), Leven Leatherbury; 77(t), H. Armstrong Roberts, Inc.; 93, Zig Leszczynski/Animals, Animals.

UNIT 4: Page 107(tl), 107(cl), Clint Clemens, Boston; 107(bl), Robert Brenner; 107(r), Aldo Tutino; 110(l), Bettmann Archive; 110(tr), Allen Lee Page/The Stock Market of NY; 110(br), Myles E. Baker; 112, Marimekko's *Snow Flower* by Dan River, Inc.; 114(t), 114(b), Sydney D. Brown; 115(t), Leven Leatherbury; 120, Walter Free/Camerique; 121 (tr), Heidecker/Camerique; 122(l), Art Resource, NY; 122(r), Jim Kransberger; 124, Bobby Hanson; 126(l), Tom Myers; 126(tr), Joseph A. DiChello, Jr.; 126(br), E.R. Degginger; 130, Bob and Ira Spring; 132, Katrina Thomas/Photo Researchers, Inc.; 133, Leven Leatherbury.

Art in Action

Guy Hubbard

Indiana University

Contributing Educators:

D. Sydney Brown
Lee C. Hanson
Barbara Herberholz

CORONADO PUBLISHERS

San Diego   Orlando   Dallas   Chicago

Requests for permission to make copies of any part of the work should be mailed to: Coronado Publishers, Inc., 1250 Sixth Avenue, San Diego, CA 92101

ACKNOWLEDGMENTS

For permission to reprint copyrighted material, grateful acknowledgment is made to the following:

DOUBLEDAY AND COMPANY: "Mice" by Rose Fyleman from *Fifty-One New Nursery Rhymes* by Rose Fyleman, copyright 1931, 1932 by Doubleday.

Printed in the United States of America   ISBN 0-15-770046-1(2)

8901 062 9876543

Table of Contents

Unit 1

Art All Around

What does art mean to you?
What kinds of art can you do?

Where can you find art?

Art is all around you.
Art is everywhere.

1 Art in Your World

Looking and Thinking

There are many ways to tell about your world.

You can look.
You can sing or shout.
You can write or dance.
You can paint or draw.

See the **shapes**.
See the **lines**.
And see the **spaces** in between.
See and feel the **textures**.

Artists can make
pictures to tell us what
they see, feel, and think.

Edgar Degas, Ballerina, *San Diego Museum of Art.*

3

2 Straight Lines

Looking and Thinking

Straight **lines** can be short or long.

They can go up and down.

They can go from side to side.

They can be **diagonal**.

When the ends of two straight lines meet, they
make an **angle**.

Ben Shahn, Still Music, Tempera on cloth mounted on panel, 48" x 83½". The Phillips Collection, Washington, D.C.

How did this artist use lines and angles?

Making Art

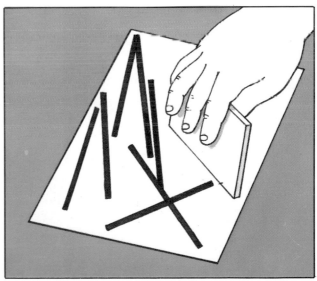

We can print straight lines and angles with strips of cardboard.
We can make pictures and designs with lines and angles.

3 *Lines That Curve*

Looking and Thinking

Lines can curve and flow and swirl.
Lines show us the edges of things.

Harry Vital, Birds and Cattle, 1972, Oil. Permanent Collection, Texas Southern University, Houston, Texas.

Vincent Van Gogh, Dr. Paul Gachet, 1890. Jeu de Paume, Paris.

Artists use curving lines in many ways.
How are these two pictures different?
How are they alike?

Making Art

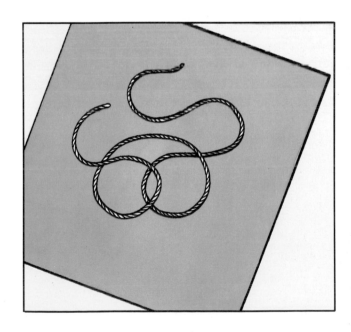

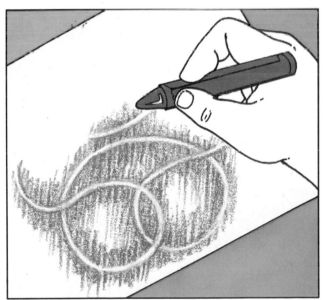

We can make curving, looping lines with string.

We can make a rubbing with a crayon.

4 Lines Tell a Story

Looking and Thinking

Franz Marc, The Large Blue Horses, 1911, Oil on Canvas, 40¾" x 70⅞". Walker Art Center, Minneapolis; Gift of the Gilbert M. Walker Fund.

The horses look strong and soft.
The artist used lines to show this.

Look at the lines in this picture.
What feelings do the lines show?

Making Art

You can make your lines dance.

Can you hear the song?

1. Use the side of a crayon.
   Let the crayon move to music.

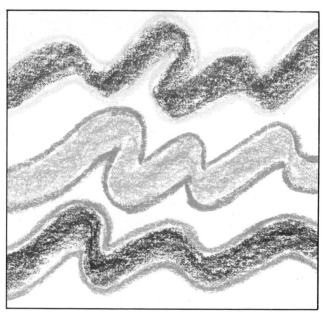

2. Make many lines.

3. Take another crayon. Use the
   point. Follow the first lines.

4. Follow with another line.

5 Lines Make Shapes

Looking and Thinking

Marsden Hartley, American, 1877-1943,The Aero, c. 1914, Canvas, without frame, 39½" x 34½". National Gallery of Art, Washington, Andrew W. Mellon Fund.

Can you find **shapes** that are curved?
Can you find shapes that have straight sides?
Find shapes that are in front of other shapes.
Find the same shape used more than once.

Making Art

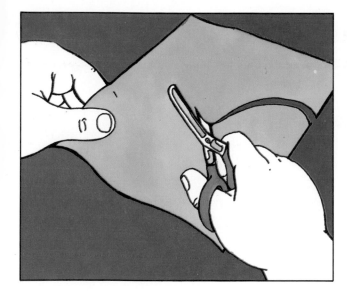

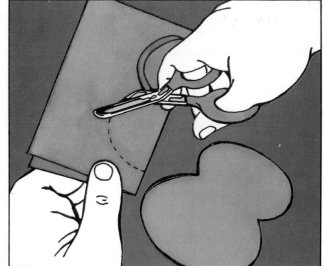

1. Use pieces of colored paper. Make curved cuts and straight cuts.

2. Fold a piece of paper in half. Cut out a shape on the fold. Unfold your shape.

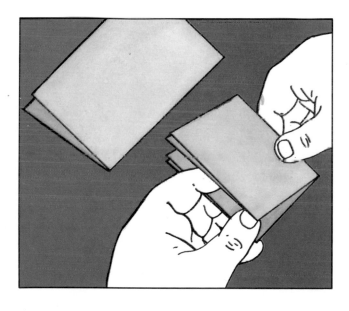

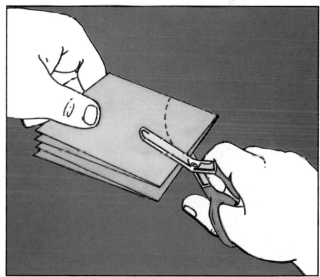

3. Fold a square in half one way and then in half the other way.

4. Cut out a curve.

Look at the shapes you have cut. Find shapes you like in your scraps, too. Choose your best shapes and paste them down. You have made a **collage**.

6 Finding Shapes

Looking and Thinking

les bêtes de la mer...
H. matisse 50

Henri Matisse (mah TEESE) made this picture. He cut shapes out of paper.

Can you see shapes of plants and fish? Look at the spaces between the shapes, too.

Which shapes do you like best?

Henri Matisse, French, 1869-1954, Beasts of the Sea, dated [19]50, Paper on canvas (collage), 116⅜" x 60⅝". National Gallery of Art, Washington, Ailsa Mellon Bruce Fund.

Making Art

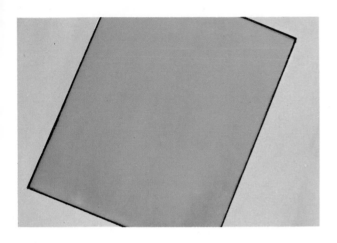

1. Choose a background paper.

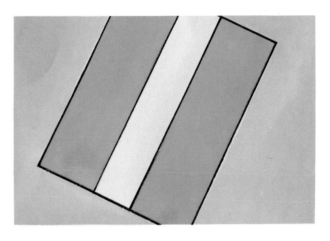

2. Choose a different color strip.

3. Cut five or more shapes.

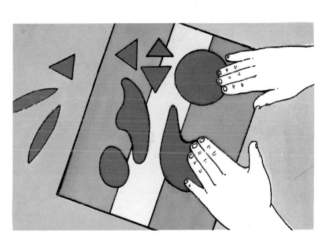

4. Arrange your shapes carefully. (Don't forget the spaces.)

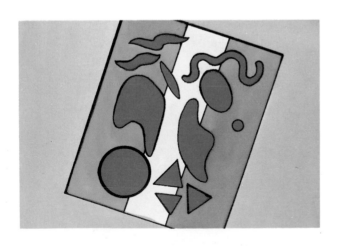

5. Paste the shapes to the background.

7 Making Shapes

Looking and Thinking

Roy Lichtenstein, The Red Horseman, *Oil and magna on canvas, 84" x 112". Photo courtesy of Leo Castelli Gallery, New York.*

Find shapes that curve.

Find two shapes next to each other.

How did the artist show movement with shapes?

Making Art

Make a **stencil**.

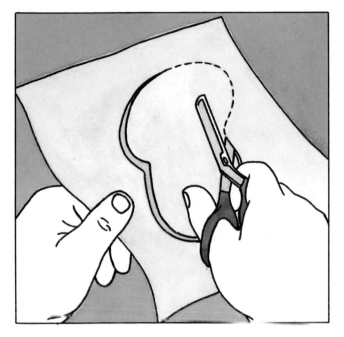

1. Cut out the stencil.

2. Color the edge.

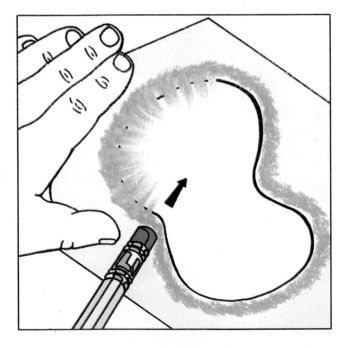

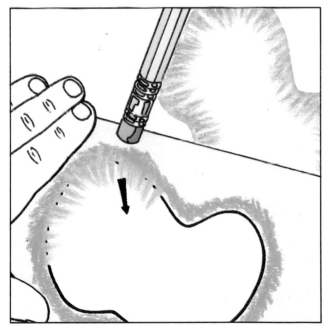

3. Hold your stencil.
   Rub an eraser into the shape.

4. Move the paper.
   Rub the eraser again.

8 Shapes Make Patterns

Looking and Thinking

Patterns are all around us.

Things that are in order make patterns.
Patterns are **rhythms** for our eyes.
These penguins make a rhythm for our eyes.

Making Art

You can make a rhythm for our eyes.

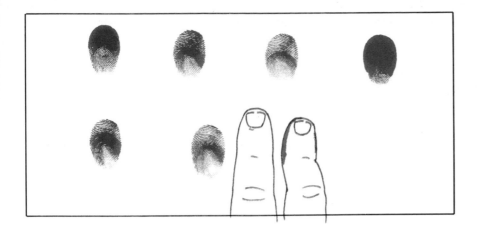

1. Use a clean finger as a space holder.

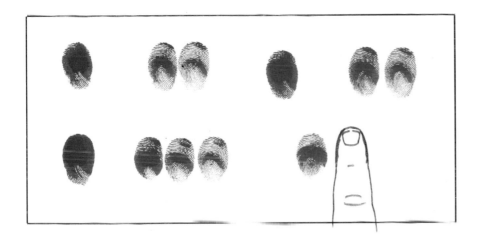

2. Try many rhythms. Can you clap them out?

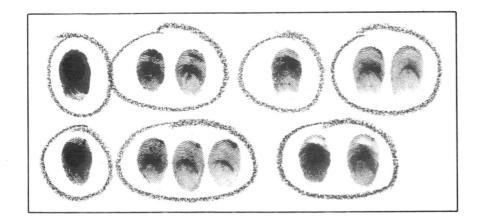

3. Put shapes around some groups.

9 Color Can Surprise You

Looking and Thinking

Can you find some new **colors**?

Making Art

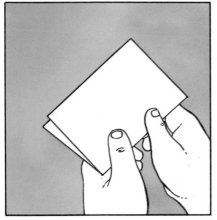

1. Fold

2. Open

3. Put on some paint.

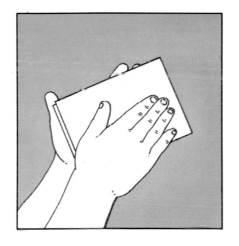

4. Fold and press.

5. Surprise

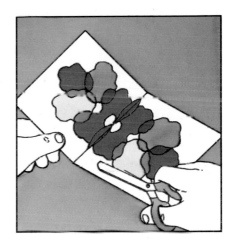

6. Trim when dry.

What new surprise colors did you find?

10 *Finding Colors You Know*

Looking and Thinking

Wassily Kandinsky, Russian, 1866-1944, Improvisation 31 (Sea Battle), 1913, Canvas, 55³⁄₈" x 47¹⁄₈". National Gallery of Art, Washington, Ailsa Mellon Bruce Fund.

Sea Battle was painted by Wassily Kandinsky (VAS uh lee kan DIHN skee). He did not paint real objects. He made a colorful painting.

Kandinsky loved bright colors. He said that blue is soft and round. He said that yellow is sharp.

The **primary** colors are red, yellow, and blue.

From these three primary colors we can mix
the **secondary** colors. They are green, orange,
and violet.

Can you find the primary and secondary colors
in *Sea Battle*?

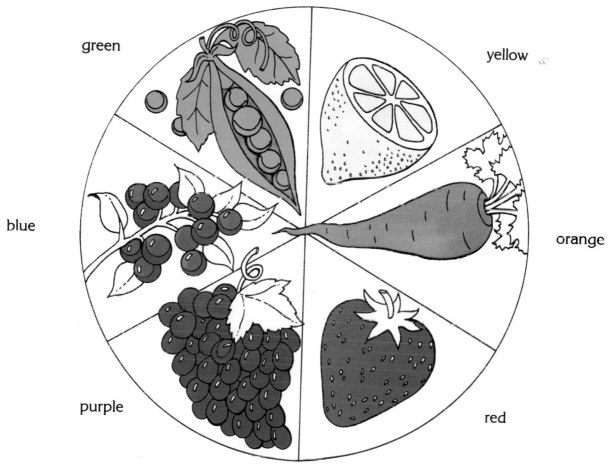

Making Art

Wet your paper on the back and front. Use a
wet sponge.

Brush some of each of the primary colors on
your wet paper. Brush some of each of the
secondary colors on your wet paper. Leave
some of the paper white.

11 *Warm and Cool Colors*

Looking and Thinking

*Claude Monet, Water Lillies, 1906, Oil on canvas,
87³/₅" x 92⁷/₁₀". Courtesy of The Art Institute of Chicago,
Mr. and Mrs. Martin A. Ryerson Collection.*

Does this painting make you
feel cool?
What colors did the artist use?

Can you feel the warm sun
shining down on these flowers?
What is the most important
color?

*Christian Rohlfs, Sunflowers, Watercolor on paper,
18³/₄" x 26¹/₄". The Detroit Institute of Arts, Gift of Mrs.
Lillian Henkel Haass and Walter F. Haass in memory of
Reverend W. F. Haass.*

Blue, green, and violet make us think of cool
   water, ice, snow, and winter winds.
Red, orange, and yellow remind us of warm
   sunny days and hot fires.
Artists use these colors to make us feel.

Making Art

Make a painting using warm or cool colors.

12 Different Colors

Looking and Thinking

Paul Cezanne, French, 1839-1906, Still Life with Pomegranate and Pears, c. 1895/1900, Oil on canvas, 18½" x 21¾". The Phillips Collection, Washington, Gift of Gifford Phillips.

What two colors did Paul Cezanne (say ZAHN)
  use in his painting?

Colors that are across from each other on the color wheel are **complements** (Lesson 10).

Making Art

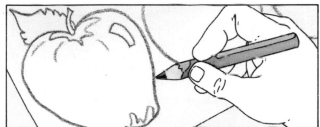

1. Draw two or three of the same kind of fruit on white paper. Draw them large.

2. Cut or tear small pieces of colored tissue paper to cover the drawing.

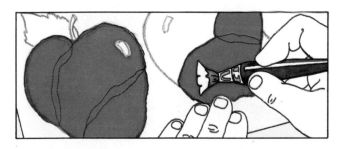

3. Use a brush and starch to make your tissue collage.

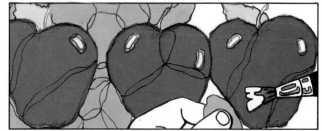

4. Cut or tear small pieces of the color complement of your fruit. Fill in all the background. Let the little pieces overlap.

13 *Finding Textures*

Looking and Thinking

What does the bottom of a tennis
  shoe feel like?

Texture is what you can feel.
How can you see texture?

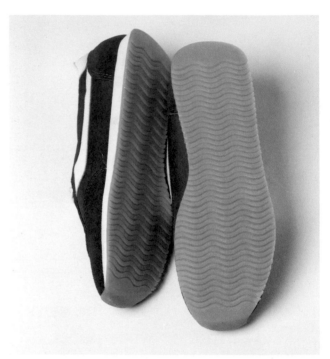

Making Art

Think of things that feel rough. Think of things
that feel smooth. What other ways can things feel?

Tear some shapes out of paper.
Use a marking pen and show texture.

14 Making Textures

Looking and Thinking

What does a scarecrow do?
How does a scarecrow dress?
How would these textures feel?

Andrew Wyeth, The Scarecrow. Private Collection.

What kind of textures did this artist paint?

Making Art

You can cut out part of a scarecrow from scraps.
You can draw the rest of your collage picture.

15 *A Sea Mural*

Looking and Thinking

Karl Hall, Bridge over Troubled Waters, 1976, Mural sketch (acrylic). Permanent Collection, Texas Southern University, Houston, Texas.

This is a **mural**. A mural is a large picture. It is sometimes painted on a wall or ceiling.

Sometimes more than one person works on a mural.
Which part of the mural do you like best? Why?

Making Art

Make a sea mural.
Look at the fish.
Think of the colors of fish.
Think of their shapes.

Exploring Art

Art in Your Community

You can find art in your **community**.
This woman is painting a mural for a children's
  museum.
Tell about other murals you have seen.

Review

Looking at Art

Franz Marc, The Large Blue Horses, 1911, Oil on Canvas, 40¾" × 70⅞". Walker Art Center, Minneapolis; Gift of the Gilbert M. Walker Fund.

Are there mostly warm colors or cool colors in
 this painting?
Do you see a pattern?
Look at the lines and shapes.
Look at the colors and textures.
What can you tell?

Unit 2

Looking More Closely

Paul Klee, Red Balloon, *1922, Oil on chalk-primed gauze mounted on board, 12½" x 12¼", The Solomon R. Guggenheim Museum, New York.*

Look at the lines and shapes.
Look at the colors and textures.
What is this a painting of?

How is this photograph like the painting?

16 *Art to Wear*

Looking and Thinking

Pende people of Zaire, Raffia costumes of Minganji Dancers. *National Museum of African Art, Smithsonian Institution, Eliot Elisofon Archives.*

How are these masks alike?
How are these masks different?

What are you like when you wear a mask?

Making Art

Make a new face for yourself.
Cut and fold paper. See what fun you can have.

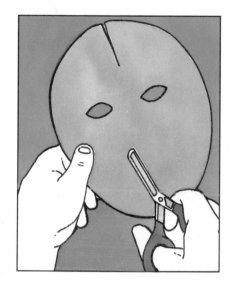

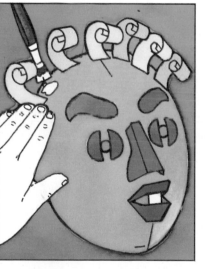

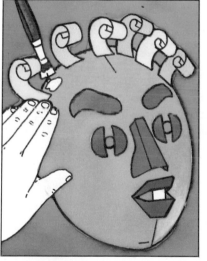

1. Cut

2. Staple

3. Score

4. Curl

5. Paste

6. What will you add?

17 Scary Faces

Looking and Thinking

Joan Miró, Spanish, Head of a Woman, 1938, Oil on canvas, 18" × 21⅝". The Minneapolis Institute of Arts, Gift of Mr. and Mrs. Donald Winston.

What do you think this
  woman is saying?
Describe the face.

What makes a face scary?
Big glaring eyes?
Lots of pointy teeth?
A warty green nose?
What else?
Look in the mirror. Make a scary face.

Making Art

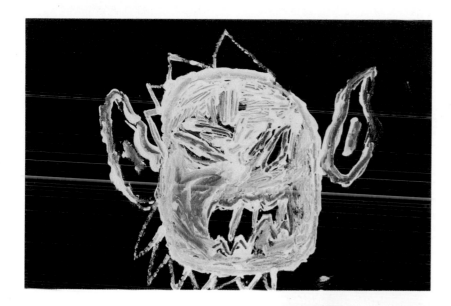

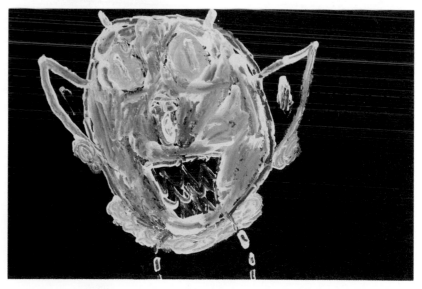

You can draw a scary face.
Dip colored chalk in white **tempera.**
Use black paper and make your face or faces
  very large.

18 *Feather Patterns*

Looking and Thinking

James Audubon, Wild Turkey, *Courtesy of The New York Historical Society, New York.*

This artist shows much fine **detail** in this bird's feathers. See the dark and light patterns that the feathers make. The patterns give the picture **unity**.

Look at the pictures of turkeys.
What shapes are repeated?
What patterns do the feather shapes make?

Making Art

Draw a turkey.
Give unity to your picture. Repeat the feather shapes.
Use a sponge brush. Put a **color wash** over
  your crayon or **oil pastel** drawing.

19 Using a Paintbrush

Looking and Thinking

Vincent van Gogh, Dutch, 1853-1890, The Auvers Stairs with Five Figures, *Oil on canvas, 20" x 28". The Saint Louis Art Museum.*

Vincent Van Gogh (van GOH) liked to use thick paint.
Can you see his brushstrokes?
What do they look like?
Can you see how he painted a color next to
   another color?
Find places where he painted a color on top of
   another color.

Making Art

Dip your brush in paint.
Paint a thick line across your paper.
Paint a thick, wavy line above or below it.
Then paint some more lines.
Use the flat side or the narrow side of your brush.

Paint some thin lines

    wavy lines

    zigzag lines

    dots

    broken lines

    lines that change from
      thick to thin

Paint in between the lines after the paint is dry.
Wash your brush in water after you use each color.
Wipe the brush dry on a damp sponge or
  paper towel.

20 *Mixing Colors*

Looking and Thinking

Georges Rouault, Profile of a Clown, *Oil on paperboard mounted on panel, 26" x 18⅞". Fanny P. Mason Fund, Museum of Fine Arts, Boston.*

The artist Rouault (roo OH) liked to use bold, black outlines.

He brushed paint inside the black lines.

Making Art

Use a piece of chalk and draw a bird, butterfly,
  or beetle.
Make your drawing touch the edges of the paper.
Brush black paint over the lines.
Dip your brush into a primary color.
Put some paint on your paper.

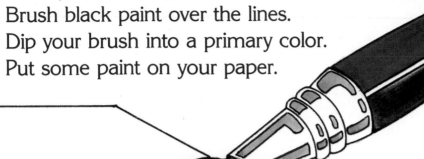

Put another primary color in the same space.

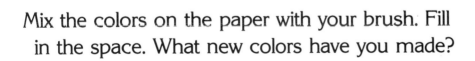

Mix the colors on the paper with your brush. Fill
  in the space. What new colors have you made?

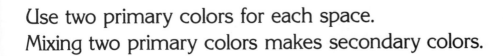

Use two primary colors for each space.
Mixing two primary colors makes secondary colors.

21 *Light and Dark Colors*

Looking and Thinking

Piet Mondrian, Horizontal Tree, 1911, Oil on canvas, 29⅝" x 43⅞" Munson-Williams-Proctor Institute, Utica, New York.

What happens when you add a little bit of a
 color to white paint?
This artist used light blue for his picture.
Light colors are called **tints**.

Look at this tree.
See how the branches reach up and out?

Making Art

1. Draw part of a tree on your paper. Make the tree touch all four sides of the paper.

2. Mix a tiny bit of a color with white paint.

3. Paint a narrow band of this tint. Paint around all the branches and trunk of your tree.

4. Make a darker tint. Paint another band up close to the first one.

5. Fill in the rest of the spaces with bands of darker tints. You have painted **negative spaces**.

6. Now paint the tree black.

22 Painting Gray Things

Looking and Thinking

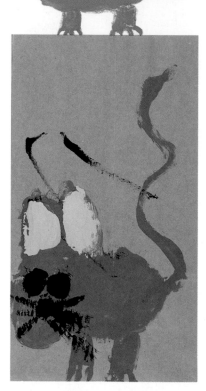

Mice
I think mice
Are rather nice.
    Their tails are long,
    Their faces small,
    They haven't any
    Chins at all.
    Their ears are pink,
    Their teeth are white,
    They run about
    The house at night.
    They nibble things
    They shouldn't touch
    And no one seems
    To like them much.
But I think mice
Are nice.

Rose Fyleman

A little green added to red makes a dull red.
A little red added to green makes a dull green.
The same amounts of red and green mixed
    make gray.
If you add white you will have a light gray.

Making Art

Think of gray things.

A Robot Party

Mice on the Run

An Elephant Parade

Paint a picture of gray things.
Fill the paper with your painting.

23 *Art That Tells Time*

Looking and Thinking

How does July make you feel?
What is fun to do in January?

Making Art

Think of all the months.

1. Make a picture for each month.

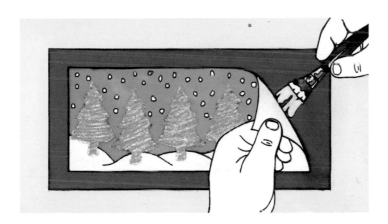

2. Paste each picture onto another piece of paper.

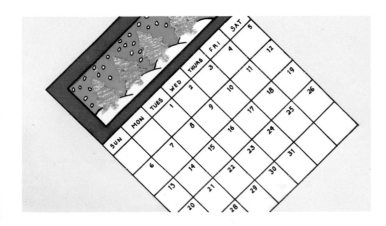

3. Paste each picture onto the right month.
   Make your calendar a present.

24 Printing with Fruit

Looking and Thinking

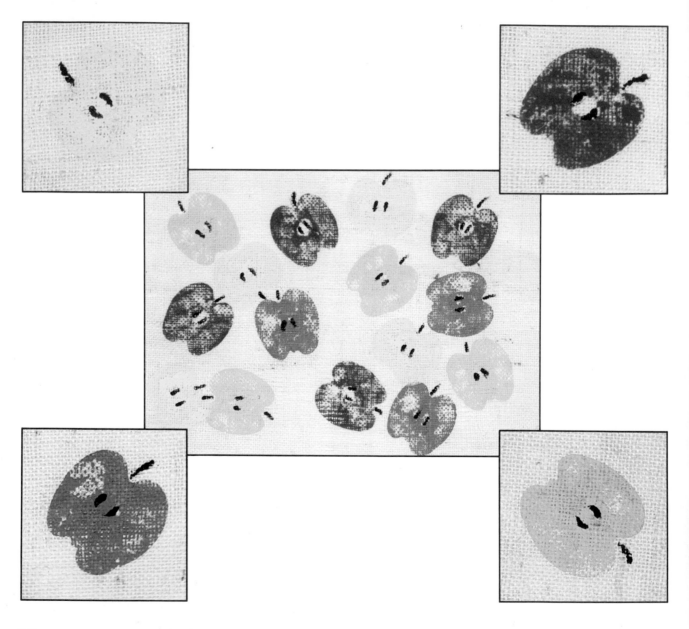

You can print with fruit.
Look at the print of the apple.
Does it look just like a real apple?
How is it different? How is it the same?

Making Art

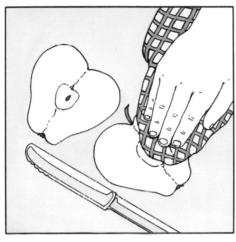

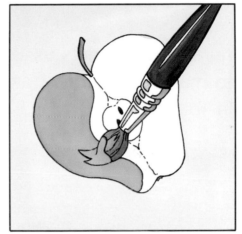

1. Dry the apple half.

2. Brush some paint onto the apple.

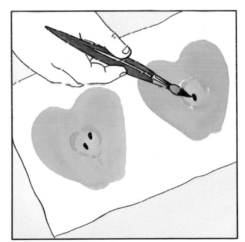

3. Press the apple on the cloth.

4. Paint some seeds.

What other foods do you think you can print with?

25 Paper Weaving

Looking and Thinking

This is a mural. The students used **paper weaving** to make the picture. Can you find weaving in your clothes?

Point to the animals in the mural. The animals are **woven**.

Making Art

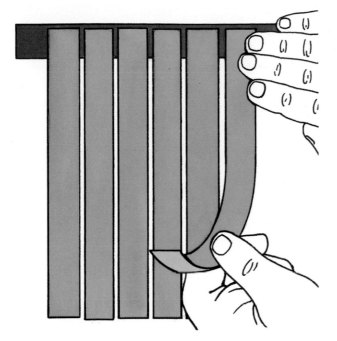

1. Put paste across the top of a piece of paper. Place strips of another color of paper close together along this pasted band.

2. Use a second color of strips. Weave one strip over and under the first strips.

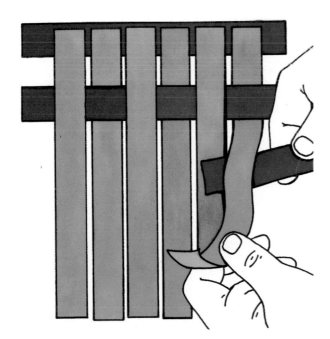

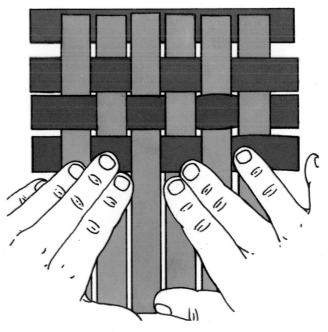

3. Weave the next strip under and over.

4. Push the strips up close against each other.

26 *Soda Straw Weaving*

Looking and Thinking

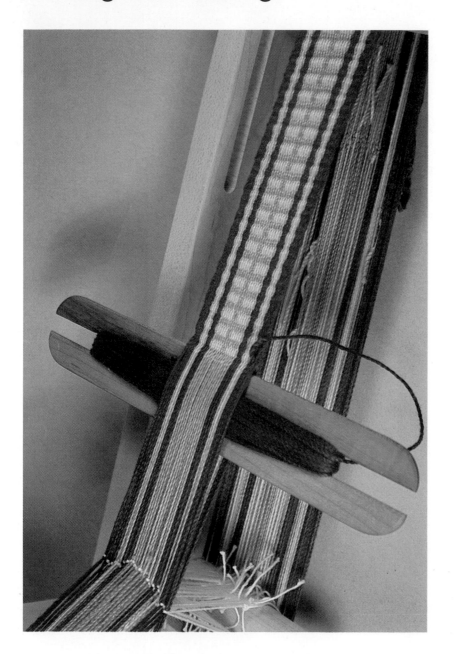

This is an **inkle loom**. Weavers have used inkle looms for hundreds of years. They make colorful bands.

Making Art

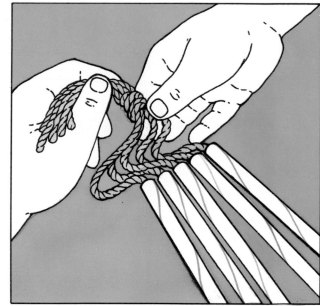

1. Cut pieces of thick yarn. Push a piece through each straw. Tie three or four knots in one end of each piece of yarn.

2. Tie all the other ends together in a big knot.

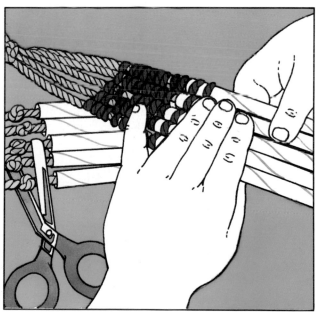

3. Weave over and under and back and forth. Use a long piece of yarn.

4. Cut the knots when you are finished. Push the weaving off the straws.

27 *A Pop Out Card*

Looking and Thinking

Children made these cards.
They used paper.
Name some things they did to make the cards.

Making Art

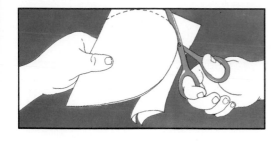

1. Fold a piece of paper. Cut out a heart.

2. Open the heart. Check its shape.

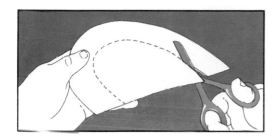

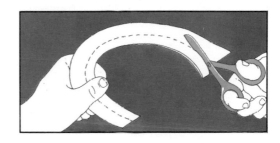

3. Fold the heart. Cut another heart from the center.

4. Cut some from the large heart.

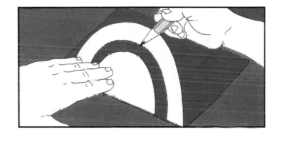

5. Trace onto another piece of paper.

6. Make a bridge.

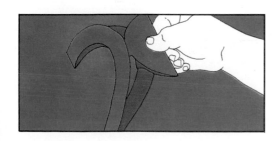

7. Cut along the lines. Fold the heart back.

8. Glue the heart onto your card.

28 Making Designs

Looking and Thinking

This **design** was made by an artist.
A machine printed the wallpaper.

Making Art

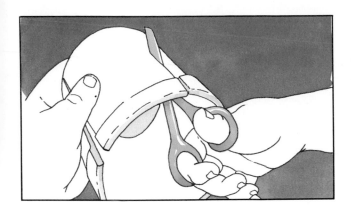

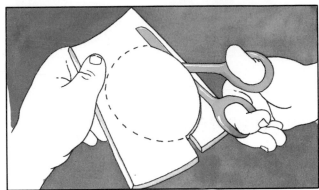

1. Cut a styrofoam cup.

2. Trace an egg shape onto the cup. Cut out the egg.

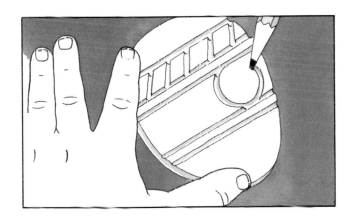

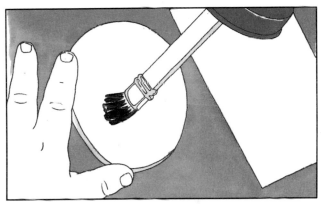

3. Make a design on the egg.

4. Put a little rubber cement on the back of the egg. Glue the egg to cardboard.

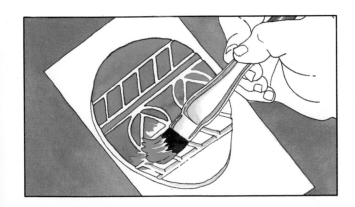

5. Brush paint on top of the egg.

6. Fold the ends of the cardboard. Print.

29 A Class Book

Looking and Thinking

Do you have a favorite book?
Who wrote it?
Who made the pictures for it?

How is this kind of book different from other
kinds of books?

Making Art

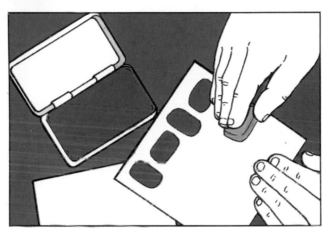

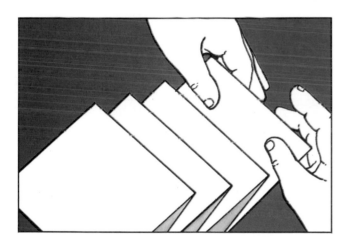

We can make a book with our own pictures
  and words.

We can **bind** it in a special way.
  It is a zigzag book.

Exploring Art

Book Jackets

Cooper Edens designed this cover for his book.
How did he make it interesting?

Look for book covers in your classroom.
Which ones do you like?
Why do you like them?

Review

Creating Art

*Georges Rouault, Profile of a Clown,
Oil on paperboard mounted on panel,
26" x 18⅞". Fanny P. Mason Fund,
Museum of Fine Arts, Boston.*

What can you tell about this painting?
Think about these things

brushstrokes   primary colors

light colors   secondary colors

dark colors

Unit 3

How Artists See

Charles Demuth, 1883-1935, Tomatoes, Peppers and Zinnias, ca. 1927, Watercolor, 17⅝" x 11½", Collection of the Newark Museum.

Do artists look at things in different ways?
What do you think artists see?

Do artists look behind and under?

Henry Moore, Reclining Figure No. 1, *1957, Bronze. Museum of Art, Carnegie Institute.*

John Singer Sargent, American, 1856-1925, The Daughters of Edward D. Boit, *1892, Oil on canvas, 87" x 87", Museum of Fine Arts, Boston, Gift of Mary Louisa Boit, Florence D. Boit, Jane Hubbard Boit, and Julia Overing Boit, in memory of their father, 1919.*

Do artists look all around?
Tell what you see.

30 *Looking at Our World*

Looking and Thinking

Georgia O'Keeffe, White Trumpet Flower, *San Diego Museum of Art Collection with Permission from Georgia O'Keeffe.*

You can look at your world in many ways.
Georgia O'Keeffe looked from very near.

Have you looked at things from very near?

Making Art

Here is an easy way to see like an artist.

1. Make a view finder like this.

2. Fold a 3" × 5" card.

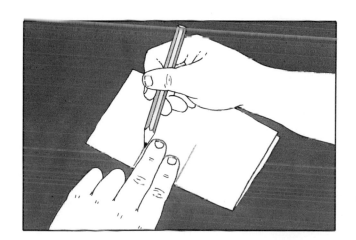

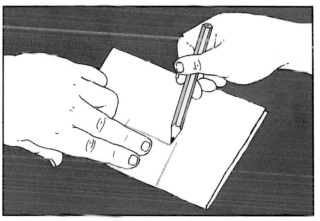

3. Mark off your fingers.

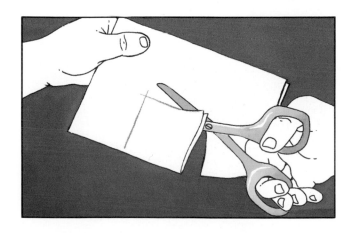

4. Cut out a square on the fold.

Looking and Thinking

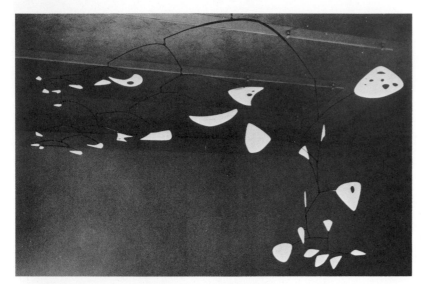

Alexander Calder, International Mobile, 1949, sheet aluminum, maximum dimensions, 20' x 20'. The Museum of Fine Arts, Houston, Gift of Dominique and John de Menil.

Japanese, The Hundred Black Crows, early Edo period, early 17th century. One of two six-fold screens; gold leaf, ink, and lacquer on paper. 61¾" (height). The Seattle Art Museum, Eugene Fuller Memorial Collection. 36.21.

Look at the **spaces** and **shapes** around you.
Spread your fingers open. Hold your fingers in
front of your eyes. Look through the spaces.

Making Art

Look at the birds on the other page.
Look at birds outside.

Tear seven bird shapes out of paper. (Do not
   draw them first.)

Paste the shapes on your paper. Think of the
   spaces, too.

32 *Looking at Lines*

Looking and Thinking

Find a straight line.
Find a wavy line.
Find other kinds of lines.
Find lines in your classroom.

Making Art

Use your birds from Lesson 31. Make some
   branches in front of your birds.

Use a crayon.

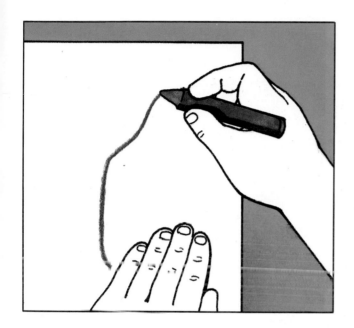

1. Draw one line.

2. Follow it with another line.
   Make a branch.

3. Do it many times.

33 *What Makes Balance?*

Looking and Thinking

Arthur Dove, Red Sun 1935, Oil on canvas, 20½" x 28". The Phillips Collection, Washington, D.C.

Balance is like a see-saw.
Pretend the painting is a see-saw.

Pablo Picasso, Two Acrobats with a Dog, 1905, Gouache on cardboard, 41½" x 29½". Collection, The Museum of Modern Art, New York. Gift of Mr. and Mrs. William A. M. Burden.

How did the artists balance color and shape?

Making Art

You can work with balance like an artist.

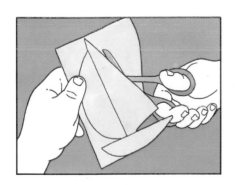

1. Cut seven sailboat shapes. Cut them different sizes.

2. Imagine a see-saw on the paper. Place two boats on one side. Do not paste them down.

3. Place other boats to make the first two balance. You do not need to use all of your boats.

34 *What Is Important?*

Looking and Thinking

George Caleb Bingham, American, 1811-1879, The Jolly Flatboatmen, Canvas 38⅛" x 48½". National Gallery of Art, Washington, Lent by the Pell Family Trust; Honorable Claiborne Pell, Trustee.

What is important?

Many things are important in drawing and painting. You are the artist. You choose the thing you want to tell about.

You can make something stand out through color. Name another way you can make something stand out.

Making Art

1. Cut 10 strips of paper in a color you like.
2. Cut a very thin strip of a different color.
3. Make a design with the strips.

35 *Things Far Away*
Things Close Up

Looking and Thinking

Edward Hicks, American 1780-1849, The Peaceable Kingdom, 1846, Oil on canvas, 24" × 31¾".
Signed: Printed on stretcher "Painted by Edward Hicks in the 66th year of his age." The Phillips
Collection, Washington, D.C.

Is the boat closer to you or is the lion closer to you?

How do you know?

Making Art

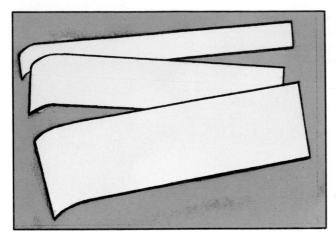

1. Use three strips of paper.

2. Use the widest strip. Draw the biggest things. Use the whole strip.

3. Use the next size strip. Draw more things. These things will be in the middle of your picture.

4. Now use the smallest strip. The things you draw on the strip will be far away on your picture.

5. Put your picture together.

36 **Spatter Painting**

Looking and Thinking

Jackson Pollock, Full Fathom Five, *1947, Oil on canvas with nails, tacks, buttons, key, coins, cigarette, matches, etc., 50⅞" x 30⅛". Collection, The Museum of Modern Art, New York, Gift of Peggy Guggenheim.*

Jackson Pollock made these paintings.
His canvas was on the floor.
How does your eye move across
  the painting?

Jackson Pollock, Number 1, 1948, 1948, Oil on canvas, 68" x 8'8". Collection, The Museum of Modern Art, New York, Purchase.

Making Art

Children made these paintings.

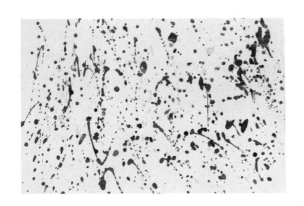 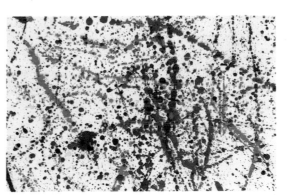

Lay a piece of white cloth or paper on the floor.
Dip your paintbrush into the paint.
Hold the paintbrush over your paper.
Do not touch the paper with the brush.
Try different motions with the brush.
Make sure to move the brush to all parts of
    the paper.

37 Artists' Pictures of Places

Looking and Thinking

Art can tell about places we know. We make
 pictures of places to share them with others.

Edward Hopper, Early Sunday Morning, *1930, Oil on canvas, 35" x 60". Collection of Whitney Museum of American Art.*

Ernst L. Kirchner, Mountain Landscape from Clavadel, *Oil on canvas, 53⅛" x 78⅛".*
Museum of Fine Arts, Boston, Arthur Gordon Tompkins Residuary Fund.

Making Art

Children made these paintings.

Draw a picture of a place where you have been.
Use crayon.

Choose bright colors. Press hard.
When you have finished, paint black or dark
  blue watercolor over your paper.

38 Paintings of Water

Looking and Thinking

Winslow Homer, American 1836-1910, Breezing Up (A Fair Wind), 1876, Canvas. 24⅛" x 38⅛". National Gallery of Art, Washington, Gift of the W. L. and May T. Mellon Foundation.

Joseph Mallord William Turner, British, 1775-1851, The Junction of the Thames and the Medway, c. 1805-1806, Canvas, 42¾" x 56½". National Gallery of Art, Washington, Widener Collection.

How are these paintings alike?
How are they different?
What can you tell about the water in these paintings?

Making Art

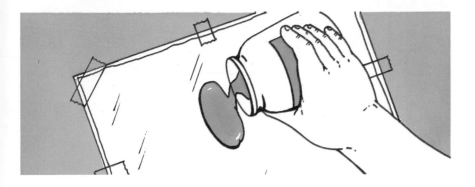

1. Tape plastic wrap to the table.
2. Pour paint.

3. Smooth out the paint with your hand.
4. Make wave motions with your hands
   and fingers.

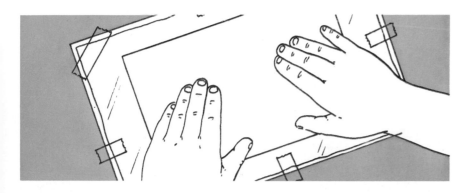

5. Work until you like what you've done. Lay a
   paper over your picture.
6. Gently rub the paper. Then pick it up by
   its edges.

39 Artists
Paint People

Looking and Thinking

Amedeo Modigliani, Italian, 1884-1920, Woman with Red Hair, 1917, Canvas, 36¼" x 23⅞". National Gallery of Art, Washington, Chester Dale Collection.

This is a **portrait**. A portrait is a picture of someone.

Which shapes in this portrait do you like best?

Making Art

Sit face to face. Find a partner.
Look at the shapes before you.
Draw what you see.

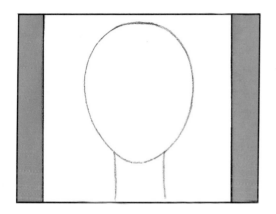

1. Make an egg.
   Put on a neck.

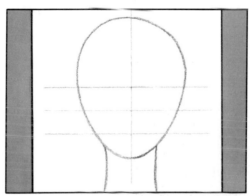

2. Draw lines lightly.
   Make three
   even spaces.

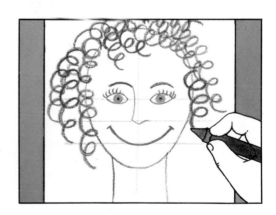

3. Look at your neighbor.
   Draw hair. Do all
   the rest.

40 *Ready for Action*

Looking and Thinking

This artist painted people playing a game.
How did he show action?

Philip Evergood, Sunny Side of the Street. In the collection of The Corcoran Gallery of Art, Museum Purchase, Anna E. Clark Fund, 1951.

Our knees bend. Our elbows bend. Our legs
bend at our hips. Our arms reach out from our
shoulders. Where else do our bodies move?

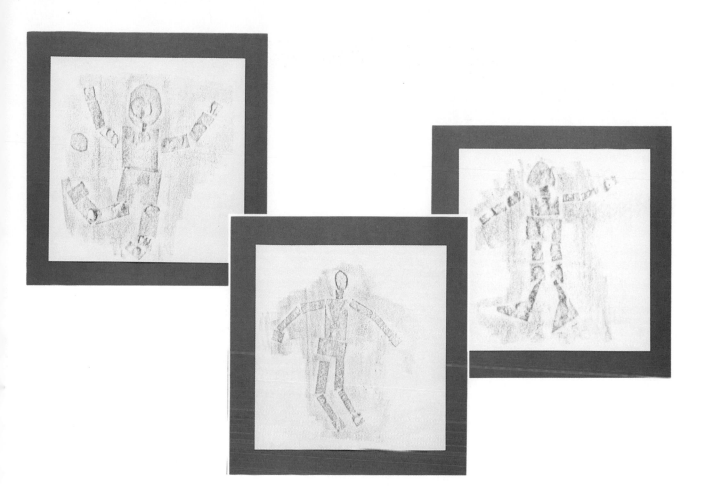

Making Art

1. Use some wide and some narrow strips of paper.

2. Cut out 16 pieces to make a **figure**.

3. Put these 16 pieces on a piece of paper. The pieces should touch each other.

4. Make your figure show action. Paste the 16 pieces down.

5. Put a thin paper over your figure. Use the side of a crayon.

6. Rub it over your figure. Press hard on the edges of your figure.

41 A Still Life

Looking and Thinking

Roy Lichenstein, Still Life with Crystal Bowl, *1973, Oil and magna on canvas, 52" x 42". Collection of Whitney Museum of American Art, New York.*

This is a painting of a group of fruit.
Artists call a group like this a **still life**.

Artists like to tell us about the shape and color of common things. They like to help us see in new ways.

Making Art

Using colored chalk is a way to show shape
  and color in a still life.

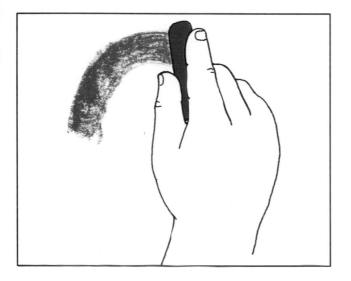

1. Use the side of your chalk.

2. Look at the shapes in your
   still life.

3. Start with big shapes.

4. Use your chalk lightly until you
   like the shapes you make.

5. You may want to add ink lines or paint lines.

Which of your shapes do you like the best?

42 Drawing Outlines

Looking and Thinking

Alexander Calder, Calder's Animals, 1931, Drawings for Aesop's Fables. Rare Books and Manuscripts Division; The New York Public Library; Astor, Lenox and Tilden Foundations.

Alexander Calder drew these animals.
They were drawn with one long line.

Making Art

1. Look at the outline of the lion. Look at objects around your classroom. Choose an object to draw.

2. Do not look at your paper. Draw with a marking pen.

3. Make one long line. Do not lift your pen off the paper.

43 *Clay People*

Looking and Thinking

Elie Nadelman, Man in the Open Air, *c. 1915, Bronze, 54½" high, at base 11¾" x 21½". Collection, The Museum of Modern Art, New York. Gift of William S. Paley (by exchange).*

Abastenia St. Leger Eberle, Roller Skating, *Before 1909, Bronze 13" x 11¾" x 6½", Collection of the Whitney Museum of American Art.*

Look at these **sculptures** of people.

Look at the man's arms and legs.
Stand like he is standing.
Look at the girl roller skating.
Why does she look like she's moving?

Sculpture has **form**.

Making Art

Look closely at people.
See how they sit.
See how they move.

Make a sculpture.
Think about forms.

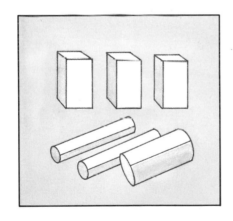

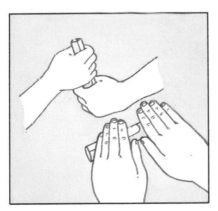

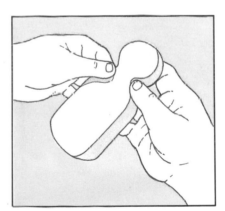

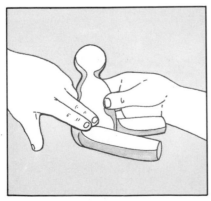

44 Salt Heads

Looking and Thinking

Children made these salty figures.
What kinds of things did the children add to
  the figures?
How do you think they made the hair?
How do you think they made the faces?

Making Art

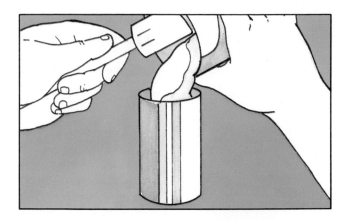

1. Fill a tube with **salt ceramic**.

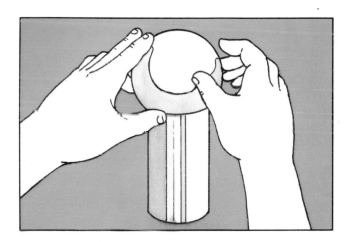

2. Make a head on top.

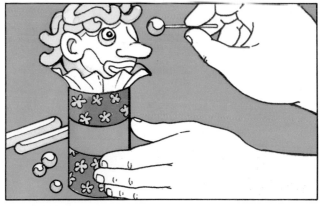

3. Practice rolling the ceramic.

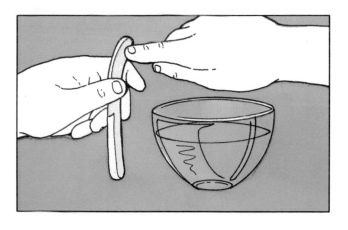

4. Make the little pieces of ceramic wet.

5. Use toothpicks to make the pieces stick onto the head.

What will you use to make clothes and hair?

45 Faces on Your Fingers

Looking and Thinking

Can you see how the paper was folded to make
  a hand puppet?

How are the two puppet faces different?

Making Art

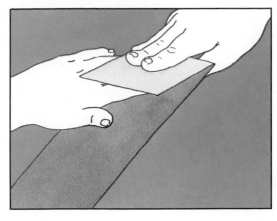

1.

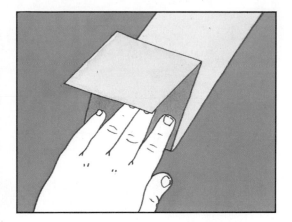

2.

3.

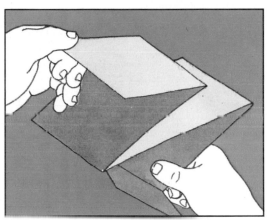

4.

5.

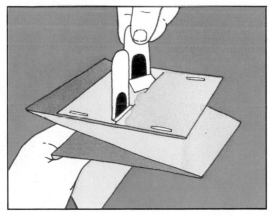

6.

Can you point to the picture that shows the
  finger pockets being made?

46 Puppets You Can Eat

Looking and Thinking

Charlie McCarthy, Kermit the Frog, Howdy Doody, *puppets. National Museum of American History, Smithsonian Institution, Washington, D.C., Reproduced with permission of the Bergman Foundation (Charlie McCarthy). KERMIT THE FROG © Henson Associates, Inc., 1980. Reprinted by Permission. The National Broadcasting Company, Inc. (Howdy Doody).*

These are famous puppets.
What do you like about puppet shows?

Making Art

Choose a fruit or vegetable.
A potato, lemon, or apple will work.

Push a stick into the fruit or vegetable.

Use sliced carrots, celery, raisins, and other
foods to make the face.

47 A Puppet Show

Looking and Thinking

Look at the puppet theater.
Where do the people sit?
Where do the puppets go?

Making Art

1. Make some puppets.
2. Make a theater.
3. Think of a problem the puppets have.
4. Think of other puppets to help.
5. Think of an ending.
6. Make your puppets move and talk.

Exploring Art

Art Careers

This is Jane Rice. She is the **deputy director** of the San Diego Museum of Art.

There are many careers in art. Name some other careers you can think of.

Review

Knowing About Art

Edward Hicks, American 1780-1849, The Peaceable Kingdom, 1846. Oil on canvas, 24" x 31¾". Signed: Printed on stretcher "Painted by Edward Hicks in 66th year of his age." The Phillips Collection, Washington, D.C.

Tell what you know about this painting.
Think of these things
   space   balance   shape   line

What kind of art do artists make?
What do they show in their art?
What kinds of things do they tell about?

Unit 4

Thinking Like an Artist

Charles Sheeler, The Artist Looks at Nature, 1943, Oil on canvas, 21" x 18". Courtesy of The Art Institute of Chicago, Collection of the Society of Contemporary American Art Gift, 1944.32.

Artists think in new ways.
They play with ideas.

American Cocktail Mixer, *Plated silver. Cooper-Hewitt Museum, New York.*

What were these artists thinking?
Were they thinking about color?
Were they thinking about shape?

Making Things Change

Looking and Thinking

You are an artist.
You are **creative**.
When you are creative, you show us
  something new.

You show us something you know.

Think of things you know.
Think of ways to change them.

Making Art

Be creative.

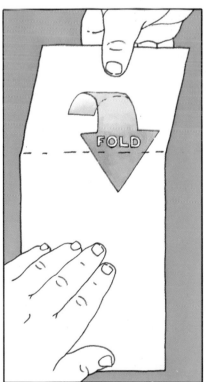

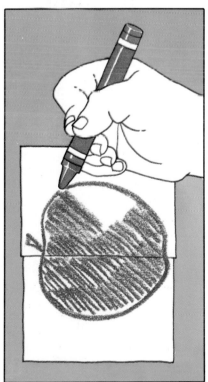

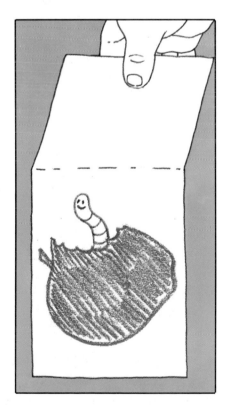

Unfold the paper. Show how your drawing changes.

49 About Artists

Looking and Thinking

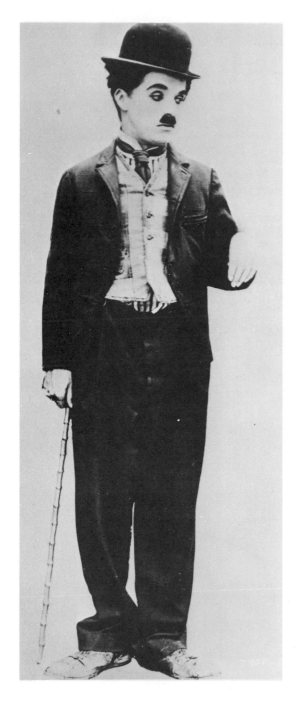

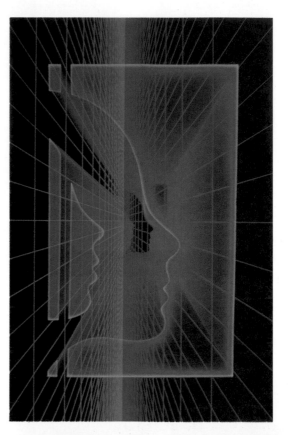

Artists made these things.

Making Art

You are an artist.
Help others see what you see.
Make a map of your school.

Take your viewfinder.

Walk around your school.
Find shapes,
    lines,
    colors,
    spaces,
    textures.
Show the places on your map where you
found them.

50 *Art in Your Home*

Looking and Thinking

Artists use shape, line, texture, and color.
Artists make things that you can use.

Making Art

Be a fabric artist.

1. Make two straight lines. Join the lines with a curve. Cut out the shape. Tape where you cut.

2. Use crayons or marking pens. Pick two bright colors. Color in your shape. Use one color. Move the shape and color again.

3. Choose another color. Color around the shape. Use rhythm (Lesson 8).

51 $\overset{A}{\text{Mosaic}}$

Looking and Thinking

This is a **mosaic**.

Small pieces of glass and clay put together
  make the design.

Making Art

You can make a mosaic with paper.

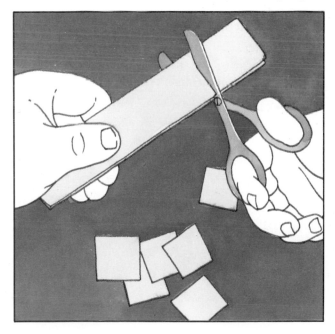

1. Cut paper into small squares.
   First cut the paper into strips.
   Then cut the paper into squares.

2. Sort the different colors.
   Put each color in its own jar.

52 *A Picture for a Poem*

Looking and Thinking

The gingham dog and the calico cat
Side by side on the table sat

Do you have a stuffed animal?
Can you tell about it?

These are collages about a poem.

Making Art

Make a collage about a poem.
Think of all the parts of the poem.

53 *Art in the Imaginary World*

Looking and Thinking

Marc Chagall, The Red Rooster, Cincinnati Art Museum, Bequest of Mary E. Johnston.

This artist shows us a rooster.

Making Art

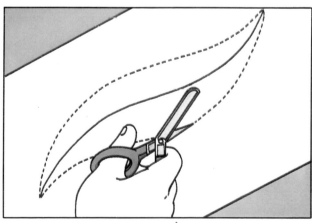

Make a rooster out of paper.

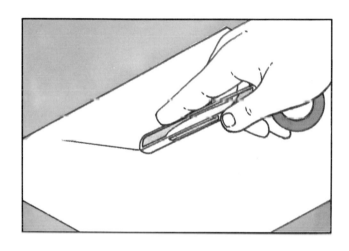

1. Draw a line with closed scissors.

2. Make a triangle for the head.

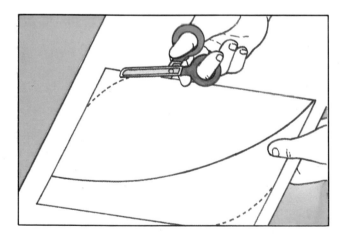

3. Make a rectangle for the body.

4. Make a leaf shape for tail feathers.

54 Art from Paper

Looking and Thinking

Look at the butterfly's wings.

Making Art

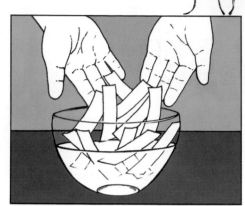

1. Cut a shape.

2. Soak some paper in paste or cornstarch.

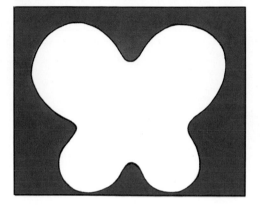

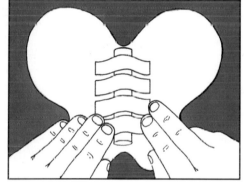

3. Fold three papers for body parts.

4. Cover with strips.

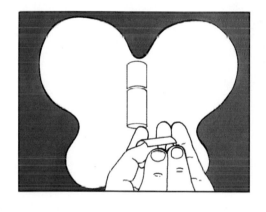

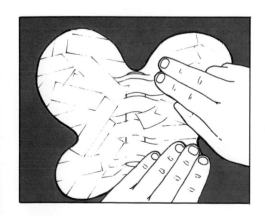

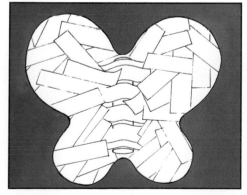

5. Cover the wings.

6. Smooth.

55 *Different Sculptures*

Looking and Thinking

Alexander Calder, Le Grande Vitesse, 1969, environmental sculpture, painted corten steel, 40' x 52' x 25'. Grand Rapids, Michigan.

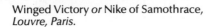

Winged Victory *or* Nike of Samothrace, *Louvre, Paris.*

These are **sculptures**.

Sculpture is art to feel, to touch, and to walk
around. You can see shadows play with sculpture.

Look at *Falling Shoestring Potatoes.*
How is it like the other sculptures?
How is it different?
Claes (klaws) Oldenburg made it. He helped
  change our ideas about sculpture.

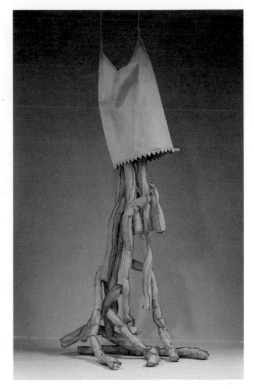

Claes Oldenburg, Falling Shoestring
Potatoes, *1965, Painted canvas, kapok,
108" x 46" x 42". Walker Art Center,
Minneapolis, Gift of the T. B. Walker
Foundation.*

Making Art

1. Be an artist. Make your own
   giant soft sculpture.

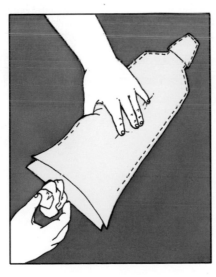

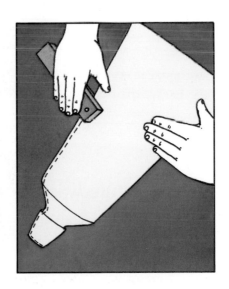

2. Draw your idea on
   two sheets of
   paper. Cut out
   your drawing.

3. Staple around the
   sides. Leave an
   opening.

4. Stuff paper into
   your sculpture.
   Staple the
   opening.

56 *Wood Scrap Sculpture*

Looking and Thinking

Joanne Syrop, Throne I, *Courtesy of the artist.*

This sculpture was made of wood.

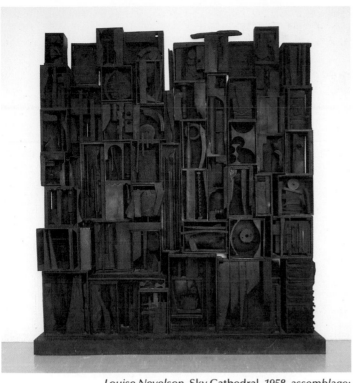

How is this sculpture like the other one?

How is it different?

Louise Nevelson, Sky Cathedral, 1958, assemblage: wood construction painted black, 11'3½" x 10'¼" x 18". Collection. The Museum of Modern Art, New York. Gift of Mr. and Mrs. Ben Mildwoff.

Making Art

What will you make with your scraps of wood?

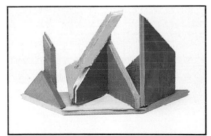

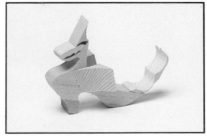

Use glue to hold the scraps together.
Let the sculptures dry overnight.
Will you paint your sculpture?

57 *Art to Live In*

Looking and Thinking

Architecture can mean places where people
   live. Or it can mean places where people play.

Making Art

Have you played in fun places?
You can be an **architect** and build places to play.
Make stairs and slides. Make caves and walls.
Make towers and tunnels.
Choose your colors carefully.

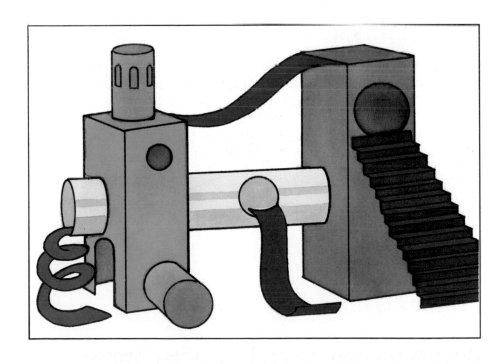

Make one piece to show how tall you would be.

58 *Art in Illustrations*

Looking and Thinking

An **illustrator** is a kind of artist.
An illustrator makes pictures to explain
  something or to tell a story.

Norman Rockwell was a famous illustrator. He
  painted pictures for magazine covers.

128

Making Art

There are many ways to make an illustration.
You can draw or paint your illustration.

1. Think of something you would like to illustrate.
   Do you want to make a picture of a part of
     a story?
   Do you want to make a book jacket?
   Do you want to make a cover for a magazine?

2. Paint or draw your illustration.

59 Art in Gardens

Looking and Thinking

Pretend you are in this garden.
Where would you walk first?

People use art to make land more beautiful.

Making Art ◇ THINK SAFETY

You can make a garden in a shoebox. This is
  called a **diorama**.

Go on a walk.
Find some things you would like to put in
  your garden.

60 An Art Show

Looking and Thinking

This is an art show.
Artists are sharing what they have done.

You have learned many ways to make art.
What do you like to do best?

Making Art

You can have an art show.

Everybody has a different way to tell about things.
You have something to share with other people.

Exploring Art

Summer Artwork

What kinds of art would you like to do this
   summer?
Why? Where are places you can work on art
   this summer?

Review

Making Up Your Mind About Art

Wassily Kandinsky, Open Green, 1923, Oil on canvas, 38¼" x 38¼". The Norton Simon Foundation.

This is called *Open Green.*

There is a painting in your book by this same
  artist.

Can you find the painting? Tell what you know
  about the artist.

Are the two paintings alike? How are they
  different?

Do you like *Open Green?* Why?

Acknowledgments

We gratefully acknowledge the valuable contributions of the following artists, consultants, editorial advisors, and reviewers who participated in the development of this book: Ruth Jones and C.J. Greenwald, teachers, St. Luke's Lutheran Day School, La Mesa, CA; Mirta Golino, art educator and editorial advisor, San Diego; Jeff Jurich, animator and writer, Celluloid Studios, Denver; Dennis Smith, sculptor, Highland, UT; Virginia Gadzala, costume designer, San Diego; Phyllis Thurston, former Art Supervisor, Pinellas County School District, Clearwater, FL; Judy Chicago and Mary Ross Taylor, Through the Flower, Benicia, CA; Andrew Blanks, Jr., art teacher, Johnston Middle School, Houston; Barbara Pearson Roberts, teacher, Sabal Palm Elementary School, Tallahassee; Shirley and Terry McManus, puppetry consultants, "Puppets Please," San Diego; Dr. Wayne Woodward, associate professor of art education, Georgia Southwestern College; Mary Riggs of Riggs Galleries, San Diego; Anna Ganahl, Director of Public Relations, Art Center College of Design, Pasadena; Françoise Gilot, artist, La Jolla, CA; Leven C. Leatherbury, independent consultant in art education, San Diego; Betty Cavanaugh, curriculum consultant in art education, Upland, CA; Joel Hagen, artist and writer, Oakdale, CA; Kellene Champlin, Art Supervisor, Fulton County Schools, Atlanta; Mar Gwen Land, art teacher, Montgomery Jr. High School, San Diego; LaRene McGregor, fiber artist, McKenzie Bridge, OR; Norma Wilson, former art teacher and editorial advisor, San Diego; Dr. Ann S. Richardson, Supervisor of Art, Foreign Languages, and Gifted and Talented Education, Charles County Public Schools, La Plata, MD; Talli Larrick, educator and writer, El Cajon, California; Mary Apuli, Coordinator of Elementary Program, Indiana School District No. 16, Minneapolis; Carol Widdop-Sonka, artist and writer, San Diego; Virginia Fitzpatrick, art educator and writer, Bloomington, IN; Evelyn Ackerman, artist, Era Industries, Culver City, CA; Judy Kugel, teacher trainer for Learning to Read Through the Arts, New York City; Arlie Zolynas, educator and author, San Diego; Nancy Remington, Principal, Sacramento County Day School, Sacramento; Kay Alexander, Art Consultant, Palo Alto School District, Palo Alto, CA; Billie Phillips, Lead Art Supervisor, St. Louis Public Schools, St. Louis; Sister Marie Albert, S.S.J., Principal, St. Callistus School, Philadelphia; Robert Vickrey, artist, Orleans, MA.

We especially appreciate the students from the following schools who contributed the student art reproduced in this series: O.H. Anderson Elem. School, Mahtomedi, MN; Atkinson Elem. School, Barnesville, MN; W.D. Hall Elem. School, El Cajon, CA; Idlewild Elem. School, Memphis, TN; Irving Elem. School, St. Louis, MO; MacArthur Elem. School, Indianapolis, IN; Oakwood Elem. School, Knoxville, TN; John Roe Elem. School, St. Louis, MO; Taylors Falls School District #140, Taylors Falls, MN; Washington Elem. School, Pomona, CA; Enterprise Elem. School, Enterprise, FL; Kellogg Elem. School, Chula Vista, CA; Learning to Read Through the Arts, New York, NY; Lewis School, San Diego, CA; Woodcrest Elem. School, Fridley, MN; Westwood Elem. School, San Diego, CA; Independent School District #16, Minneapolis, MN; St. Luke's Lutheran Day School, La Mesa, CA; Country Day School, Sacramento, CA; Budd School, Fairmont, MN; Park Terrace Elem. School, Spring Lake Park, MN; Audubon Elem. School, Baton Rouge, LA; Chilowee Elem. School, Knoxville, TN; Logan Elem. School, San Diego, CA; Grassy Creek Elem. School, Indianapolis, IN; Earle Brown Elem. School, Brooklyn Center, MN; Jefferson Elem. School, Winona, MN; Calvert Elem. School, Prince Frederick, MD; Barnsville Elem. School, Barnsville, MN; Ridgedale Elem. School, Knoxville, TN; Children's Creative and Performing Arts Academy, San Diego, CA; Steven V. Correia School, San Diego, CA; Walnut Park Elem. School, St. Louis, MO.

Although it is impossible to acknowledge all the contributors to this project, we express special thanks for the generous efforts of the following individuals: Janet Reim, Gail Kozar, Rae Murphy, Jan Thompson, Gerald Williams, Timothy Asfazadour, Judy Cannon, Helen Negley, Crystal Thorson, Rachelle and Tyler Bruford, Mary Bluhm, David Zielinski, David Oliver, Daniel and Carl Bohman, Anne G. Allen, Bao Vuong, Gail W. Guth, Signe Ringbloom, Claire Murphy, Joan Blaine, Patrice M. Sparks, and Larke Johnston.

Coronado Staff: Marsha Barrett Lippincott, Level One Editor; Janet Kylstad Coulon, Level Two Editor; Deanne Kells Cordell, Level Three Editor; Carol Spirkoff Prime, Level Four Editor; Patricia McCambridge, Level Five Editor; DeLynn Decker, Level Six Editor; Janis Heppell, Project Designer; Lisa Peters, Designer; Myrtali Anagnostopoulos, Designer; Debra Saleny, Photo Research.